A TASTE OF HUNGARY

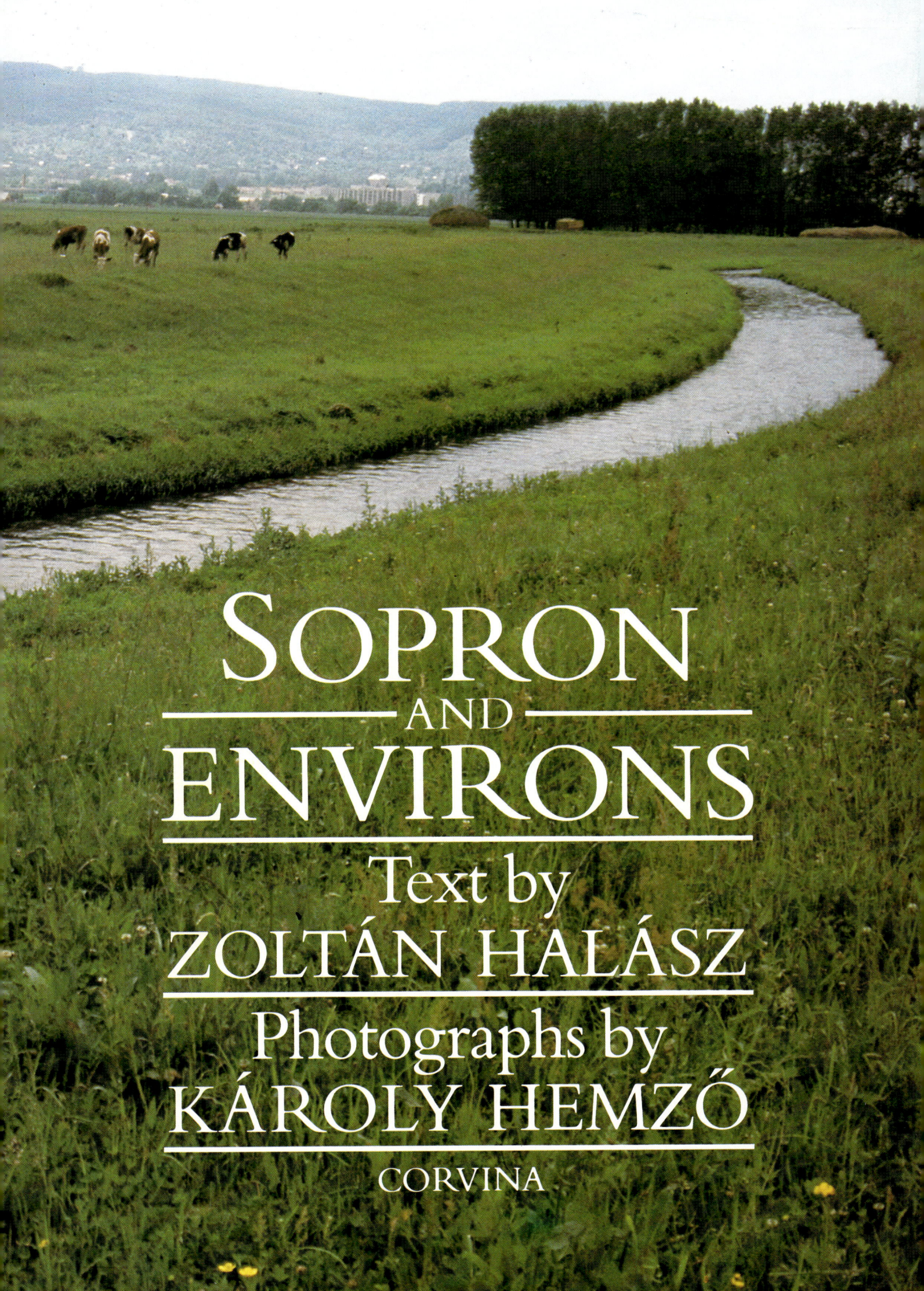

Sopron and environs

Sopron is bordered in the southwest by the foothills of the Alps which extend all the way into Hungary. These hills are little more than gentle elevations, really, the highest peak reaching a level of only 558 metres. They taper off towards the south and east and on the gentle slopes stretch centuries-old chestnut trees, vineyards, and fruit orchards for as far as the eye can see. Also containing pine, beech, and oak forest harbouring abundant game, among them deer and wild boar, this region of Hungary is truly the front yard of the Alps. The Sopron countryside is blessed and fortunate, not only with respect to its natural endowments but also because it has somehow always escaped the vicissitudes of history. The Turks were halted just short of the area, and during the Kuruc war against the Habsburgs, the battling forces spared the area. Even at the time of the Napoleonic conquests, Sopron was fortunate as Bonaparte treated the town with consideration. Tradition even has it that the Corsican took a great liking to Sopron's red wines, especially the Kékfrankos.

The preservation of Sopron's past was, however, more than just a gift of fortune, it was due also to the town's devotion to tradition. The past is visibly alive everywhere, harmoniously blending with the present. A sparkling vitality is characteristic of the town. Probably the most representative visible manifestation of this harmonious blend of past and present is the "Várostorony" or City Tower, which is also referred to as the "Fire Tower", because it served as a lookout post for centuries, enabling the detection of any fires that broke out in the town and surrounding area.

The foundations of the tower were laid in Roman times when the town was called Scarbantia. The settlement was an important one in the Danubian territory of the Roman Empire, as it lay on the Amber Route, which extended from the Mediterranean to the Baltic Sea. On top of the Roman foundation of the tower was built a cylindrical structure in the 12th or 13th century, when Sopron had already become a Royal Free Town and was receiving substantial revenue from the shipment of salt to the West. The subsequent level of the tower was built in the Renaissance style in the 16th century, under the reign of King Matthias, who spent nearly a year in Sopron, ruling the country from there during this time. The tower culminates in a Baroque structure evoking that period when Sopron's wine cellars provided Vienna with wine and Joseph Haydn conducted operas at the nearby mansion of the enlightened Prince Miklós Esterházy. All of these things are represented by the tower. From its arcaded balconies can be heard today, as in centuries past, the sound of music from brass instruments played by the "towerguards". So the tower musicians are still called, though they no longer maintain a fire watch. They are in fact Sopron residents who hold various positions in the community: one is a postman, another a clerk, and there is even a real fireman among them. They all are motivated by a love of music and a local patriotism which is so characteristic of the town's residents.

The façade of the Esterházy mansion near Sopron with the coat of arms of the Esterházy family (above).

Sopron poncichters' (bean-growers') beans, renowned for their fine flavour, are grown between the rows of grapes (right).

The Sopron City Tower (left). The Bajáns in front of the gate of their restaurant, the Halászcsárda (below). Guests are greeted in the Halászcsárda by the wooden statue of a fisherman (right). Stuffed trout, one of the culinary specialties of the Halászcsárda (lower right).

Customs past and present merge also in Sopron cooking. In the town's *poncichter* quarter (from the German word *Bohnenzüchter*), so named for Sopron's famous old bean growers, one must become acquainted with the celebrated local bean dishes. It was here, in fact, that László Baján and his wife, Marika, initiated me into the world of Sopron's culinary delights, which, like everything else in the town, have their own special history.

Sopron viniculturists discovered long ago that cabbage and beans could be planted between rows of grapes. These products, which sold extremely well at the markets of nearby Vienna, brought in a handsome income. Also, because the *poncichters* for many generations had not only an exceptionally good sense for marketing but were also very proficient at introducing improvements in farming methods and plant varieties, the beans and cabbage they transported to the markets of the "imperial capital" were of superb quality. In the evenings, the wagons left from Sopron, and next day the market women were already hawking their produce in Vienna. Those women not only knew how to grow the finest produce but also how to cook them superbly. From the tasty beans were concocted magnificent dishes, ranging from scones made from beans through mashed baked beans and bean salad up to even a bean strudel.

László Baján related all this to me in his home located in the heart of the *poncichter* quarter. Facing his house is an old medieval stone church built by the Knights Hospitallers in the early 13th century. The Baján house itself has been standing for over 400 years now. At one time it belonged to one of the Baján ancestors who owned a vineyard on the hills above, which was cultivated by successive generations of the family.

László Baján studied to be a chef and travelled extensively before returning to Sopron and finally settling down in his home town. The old house took many years of labour to restore. Gentle loving care is visible in its every detail. Under the archway of the entrance, one is greeted by the wooden statue of a fisherman, carved by a local naïve artist. In the fisherman's hand is a boat hook. Even today, fishermen in the area go out on Lake Fertő in their flat-bottomed boats in search of carp and other tasty fish; in the old days loaches lived in the lake as well. The lake is so shallow, however, that in summer one could just as easily wade across it and without a boat hook, the boats can become stuck on the lake bottom.

Baján opened his fish restaurant, the Halászcsárda, in his old house many years ago. Inside, we settled down at a table and discussed various traditional and newer fish dishes. There is an abundant supply of fish in nearby Lake Fertő: in addition to the more customary varieties consumed in Hungary, the lake now also provides *fogas* (pike-perch) and its smaller specimen, *süllő*. Hungarian and Austrian fish farmers joined efforts in full force to

colonize the lake, which is divided up between the two countries, with the famous fish. The fish then multiplied and flourished abundantly, their swimming excursions unhampered by the border running through the middle of the lake. The legendary loaches, of which—according to old-timers in the area—a delicious dish served with cabbage was prepared, have disappeared without a trace. They have been replaced by the eel, which, fortunately, has proven to be just as popular.

Choosing from among the many different fish dishes available at the restaurant is not easy, as Baján alone prepares seven kinds of fisherman's chowder (halászlé) alone! After much deliberation, I finally decided on the Sopron Fisherman's Chowder with red wine (Soproni vörösboros halászlé), which is made from carp, pike, and various smaller fish. The chowder has a subtle tartness characteristic of the Kékfrankos wine that is added to it at the end of the cooking process. Of course, my appetite and curiosity were far from satisfied. As Oscar Wilde once said: "I can resist everything except temptation." And the temptation was considerable, because Baján then entered with a bowl of Tipsy Fisherman's Chowder (korhely halászlé). This chowder is somewhat thicker than the preceding dish, and one is able to discern in its mixture of mildly pungent flavours the taste of fresh sour cream, mustard, lemon, and the dry white wine from Sopron's hillside vineyards.

Elsewhere the fish chowder would be traditionally followed by Cottage-Cheese Noodles with Crackling (tepertős túróscsusza), but in Baján's restaurant one encounters a dish which is rarely found anywhere else nowadays: Cabbage and Pike Strudel (káposztás-csukás rétes). It is a very old dish which has been handed down from father to son. The marked fish taste of the pike is counterbalanced in the strudel by the rich and mildly tangy taste of the cabbage in which it is embedded. The fish and cabbage mixture, which serves as the filling for the strudel, is rolled up in the wispy thin strudel dough and baked to a lovely golden brown. The dish is a pleasant and slightly filling one and also makes an excellent accompaniment for wine, especially the beautifully sparkling Sopron Green Veltlin (Zöldveltelini) wine that Baján serves with it. The wine is dry and smooth and goes very well with the fish pastry.

The second Baján tavern, the Bécsi-Kapu Borozó, is just a few minutes away from the Halászcsárda. However, after the hearty fish chowder and strudel, I was hardly in any condition to continue my sampling of Sopron cooking. Consequently, I decided to take a little walk and set off in the direction of the Storno House, a place which I could not possibly neglect during my visit to the area, since, like the City Tower, it represents the essence of Sopron.

The ancestors of the Storno family were of Italian and Swiss origin. They made their way from Ticino to Sopron many centuries ago. They established a chimney-sweeping business in the town, originally practising the trade themselves. Later, when they had amassed some money, they employed an army of assistants and apprentices to polish the town's chimneys, while the Stornos themselves, now a Sopron family of patricians, preferred to pursue the fine arts. Over the course of time, sculptors,

traditional fare. In the preparation of this dish, flour is first fried with a little salt but without any oil or fat, in a heavy skillet or pot to a golden brown colour. In the meantime, the beans are boiled until soft in ample water. The hot bean broth is then poured over the hot flour and sprinkled with a little oil. The beans are now added and the entire mixture is left to rest. Finally, the beans are mashed with a fork. The mash is usually browned slightly in the oven just before serving. Salad, sour cream, or buttermilk can be offered with it, but *babsterc* also makes an excellent accompaniment to any kind of meat dish prepared with sauce, including the previously mentioned Forester's Meatballs with mushroom sauce.

The other dish that I simply had to taste proved to be the highlight of the feast: Vintager's Roast *(vincellérpecsenye)*, a dish which originated in the old days when the vintagers prepared it to celebrate a good harvest. The appearance, as well as the taste, of the dish was very appetizing. The sliced leg of pork was swimming in a rich, reddish-brown sauce, which derived from the meat having been marinated in red wine. The aroma was magnificent, and I was able to detect a hint of garlic, paprika, and nutmeg in it as well. In order to adhere to *poncichter* traditions, I took bean salad as a side dish. The vinegar-onion dressing of the salad accentuated the taste of the beans excellently.

painters, artist-craftsmen and restorers emerged from among the members of the Storno family, all of whom were in agreement on one issue, namely, that the collection of art was the noblest of passions. In the meantime, the Stornos expanded and restored their house, turning it into one of the town's most beautiful Baroque mansions. Over the centuries, the Storno collection continued to grow, as more and more paintings, statues, reliefs and furniture masterpieces were added, until the family finally opened the collection to the public.

From the Storno mansion, I returned to the *poncichter* quarter with a renewed appetite to sample some of the famous Sopron bean dishes. Baján's wife, Marika, greeted me at the entrance to the Bécsi-Kapu Borozó. As an appetizer, she offered the traditional "forty drops of wine"—a glass of Sopron Kékfrankos—and some scones made from beans. The scones were light and delicate with a savoury taste of beans, eggs, and sour cream. Marika disclosed that they first prepared a yeast mixture, adding cooked beans, sour cream, eggs, salt, pepper and fat. They allowed it to rest for half an hour before mixing in the flour. Once again they left the dough to rest until well risen, then kneaded the dough, and finally rolled it out. The scones were cut out with a biscuit cutter, a bean placed on the top of each by way of decoration, and then placed in the oven to bake.

After the wine and scones, Marika brought the first course from the kitchen, which turned out to be Forester's Meatballs with Bean Mash *(erdészgombóc babsterccel)*. The dish consists of meatballs made from ground pork mixed with eggs, salt, pepper, nutmeg, and onion, over which is poured a mushroom sauce made with white wine. The Bean Mash *(babsterc)* is Sopron's most famous

The tangy taste of home-made mixed pickles is excellently suited to the Bean Mash, a Sopron favourite (above left).
A selection from the menu of the Bécsi-Kapu Wine Cellar: ingredients for Highwayman's Soup (below); Bean Mash, Forester's Dumplings, Bean Scones, and Wine Cellar Pork Roast with Bean Salad (right).

GOOSE BANQUET AT THE BAUSZES'

Saint Martin, the converter of the Gallic people to Christianity, was born, according to legend, not in Sopron, but in nearby Szombathely. (Another version locates his birthplace in the vicinity of what is today Pannonhalma.) Be that as it may, one can nevertheless find in Sopron the best goose, Saint Martin's favourite animal. And not just anywhere in Sopron either, but at the restaurant of Gyula Bausz, a renowned expert in preparing goose. His little restaurant, the Vadászkürt, is famous among Sopron gourmets for its goose dishes. I asked Bausz what prompted him to make a goose banquet every day of the year and not just on Saint Martin's Day in November, the traditional time of the goose feast. Bausz, smiled at my question and replied that it was due to the abundant, year-round supply of roasting geese in the nearby town of Sárvár. These geese, he pointed out, do not yield a heavy, fatty dish as was the case in the days of our grandparents. Noting that there were several different varieties of goose-liver dishes on the menu, I asked him from where he purchased the liver.

The Vadászkürt Restaurant, renowned for its goose dishes (above and below). One of the most important components of a goose feast: goose liver (right).

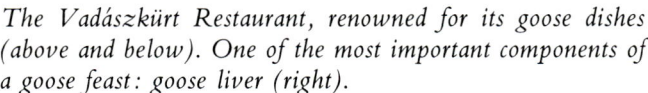

Bausz informed me that the liver is obtained from neighbouring villages where they raise geese especially for their liver. The ones having the largest livers, he added, are those fed not only with maize but also with chestnuts.

It seems that the well of history certainly runs very deep. I once read about a similar practice in the cookbook of the Roman gourmet, Apicius. The Romans fed chestnuts not only to their geese but to their pigs as well, in order to make their livers larger and tastier.

Bausz's famous goose banquet begins with a soup made from the offal of the goose, such as the neck and gizzard. The stock is seasoned, of course, with parsnips, kohlrabi, celery and other soup vegetables. The dish that followed I would call an appetizer were it not so plentiful. The goose-liver plate consisted of both grilled and fried liver slices. For my part, I prefer the grilled liver, because the delicate and rich flavours of the liver are preserved. There are others, however, who swear by the breaded, fried liver, as the crispy, egg and crumb coating provides a pleasing contrast to the softness of the liver.

The crowning glory of the banquet then followed: Stuffed Goose-Neck. The goose liver, minced goose meat, bread rolls soaked in milk, and seasonings are combined into a filling. The neck is stuffed with the mixture and baked. When done, the dish is served with mashed potatoes and steamed cabbage. I might add, moreover, that Bausz also serves a "side dish" of roast leg of goose to accompany the goose-neck. One can thus well imagine the gargantuan dimensions of the goose banquet!

THE HUNDRED-YEAR-OLD PASTRY SHOP

Ödön Hoffmann's pastry shop has been in existence for just about a century. The shop is located in a house which is far older than the establishment itself, although I did not delve into the age of the building, as one can stumble upon Roman foundations everywhere in Sopron, if one only digs deep enough. It is known for certain, however, that Ödön's great-grandfather—who was also named Ödön —founded the shop in 1888. Since then, every firstborn son has been named Ödön, and all of them have become pastry chefs. And not just ordinary pastry chefs either.

The founding Ödön Hoffmann was brought from Vienna by the restauranteur Henrik Gundel in order to prepare bon-bons, which were very fashionable at that time. In those days, Christmas trees were decorated with walnuts and hazelnuts, and the colourfully wrapped bonbons were served on china and silver dishes in the elegant salons (hence the name "salon-candy" or *szaloncukor*) of the houses of the gentry. Ödön Hoffmann made superb bon-bons, but later he also became known for his cakes,

A selection from the goose banquet: Grilled Goose Liver, Stuffed Goose Neck, Roast Leg of Goose, Fried Goose Liver (left). Bük Apple and Jam Pudding, an inexpensive but tasty sweet (above).

parfaits, and various small pastries. His son, the next Ödön Hoffmann in the line, rapidly joined the ranks of Sopron's well-to-do patricians. The Ödön Hoffmann of our time, the great-grandson of the original founder, spent his apprenticeship in Switzerland under a pastry chef by the name of Fritz Waldmeier in the city of Basel. For thirty years now, he has been the proprietor and master chef of Sopron's renowned pastry establishment. I kept trying to ferret out Ödön's baking secrets. To what does he attribute, for example, the popularity of his salted tea biscuits? No sooner are the freshly baked pastries set out, they begin to disappear, selling out within a matter of minutes.

"Hand preparation and accuracy, as well as fresh, fragrant Sopron butter", was his resounding answer.

"And the linzer wreaths, which are the finest that I've ever eaten anywhere?" I inquired.

"The same", he replied, "plus homemade apricot jam". Of course, Hoffmann's pastry craftsmanship cannot be reduced solely to such simple factors. Anyone who has ever tasted, for example, his Wild Walnut Cake *(erdei dió szelet)*, a piece of culinary poetry made from a mixture of green walnuts preserved in syrup, praline cream and marzipan, begins to sense the exquisite artistry the confectioner's trade reached in Sopron over the centuries. As for his cakes and tortes, they are veritable masterpieces. Hoffmann is a master of "sugar sculpting" or cake decorating. He creates on his cakes colourful scenes containing flowers, doves and elves, and other nostalgic scenes.

"Now that you're on to sweets, you must taste Sopron's famous Cottage-Cheese Doughnuts *(túrófánk)* as well," insisted István Gyolcs, a prominent expert on Sopron's culinary delights and the mentor of the local gastronomical association. Since such good advice could not possibly be ignored, we took leave of Hoffmann's pastry shop and headed straight for Kuruc Hill (Kurucdomb) to sample the famous pastry.

Kuruc Hill owes its name to the fact that, according to local history, during the Kuruc war against the Habsburgs at the beginning of the 18th century, the troops of General Bottyán (better known as "Bottyán the Blind") Vak's troops camped there. At that time the area was still situated well beyond the town. The Kuruc soldiers, who fought the loyal supporters of the Austrian emperor, finally gave up and left Sopron, as they were unsuccessful in their attempt to capture the town. Nevertheless, at the top of the hill still stands the old, natural stone structure which the Kuruc troops supposedly used as their quarters.

Opposite the ancient building stands a large tower, which was once a windmill. At the top of the tower, which has been restored from the ruins, the blades of the windmill turn energetically in the gentle Alpine breeze, only the mill no longer grinds flour as in the olden days. A tavern now operates on its premises. In addition to Highwayman's goulash *(betyárgulyás),* which is served with large flat noodles fried in lard, the restaurant offers such savoury specialties as Gourmet Pork Chops *(ínyencborda),* which consists of two pork chops with cheese in between, breaded and fried to a golden brown.

However, we did not visit Kuruc Hill for any of these dishes but for the aforementioned doughnuts, which they proceeded to prepare fresh for us. The plump blond cook allowed me to assist her. She mixed together the creamed cottage cheese, flour, powdered sugar, a dash of salt, and some baking soda. Rolling out the dough to finger-width thickness, she then cut out the doughnuts and fried them to a golden brown in sizzling oil. The fresh doughnuts were dusted with powdered sugar, and with some homemade apricot jam they were delivered to the table immediately.

We sat sipping wine with our doughnuts, which provided an excellent opportunity to reflect on the local wines. Sopron wines, which are noted for their fiery robust flavour and their aromatic bouquet, are as much a part of the town's atmosphere as the Gothic archways, Baroque towers, cob-

The filling for the Chestnut Roll is prepared from chestnuts grown in the surrounding area (left). A tavern now operates in the windmill of bygone days (above). Pleasantly tangy red wines of special character are made from grapes grown in the vicinity of Sopron (below left)

blestone streets, and the forests on the surrounding Lővér Mountains, not to mention the music which Haydn, Liszt, and Johann Strauss the Younger composed here. The latter supposedly composed the famous strains of "A Night in Venice" as he sat drinking in the old Golden Stag Inn (Arany Szarvas Fogadó, now the Pannonia Hotel).

Obviously, the secret of the unique character and excellent taste of Sopron wines lies in the soil of the surrounding hills and the favourable climate. But this is only part of it. Just as important are the strict sense of civic pride and morality, as well as local viniculture traditions. The utmost care has always been taken to preserve the natural quality of the wines and to prevent any undesirable practices in the area.

To guarantee the quality of Sopron wines, the town's official wine taster checks all wines offered for sale as has been the practice for centuries past. As a matter of fact, in the old days, inns and wine cellars were visited regularly by the town custodians who held a large stick in their hand, with which to prevent, if necessary, the sale of poor quality or smuggled wines. Indeed, current strict wine regulations in Hungary most probably date back to such earlier traditions.

The most famous Sopron wine is the already mentioned Kékfrankos. It is a smooth and pleasantly tangy red wine. Its must is fermented in the skin of the grapes, which gives the wine its deep burgundy colour.

White wines are less characteristic of Sopron, and very few of these are produced in the area. The Olaszrizling is an agreeable white wine with an alcohol content of 11–12°. Leányka is a dry and pleasantly tangy white wine, whilst Tramini is a soft, mild-flavoured, and well-balanced table wine.

"VASI" FLAVOURS

From Sopron the road leads southward over tree-clad hill country. The scenery along the route is truly fascinating in its diversity. At Nagycenk, an 18th-century castle surrounded by a park and stone walls comes into view. It is the former home of the famous Széchenyi family, and even today the historical residence, which is now a museum, evokes the life and work of Count István Széchenyi, the great 19th-century statesman. Recently a part of the castle has been converted into a hotel. As one continues further across the hills and woodlands, the small town of Kőszeg appears. This is an enchanting town abounding in historical monuments. Everywhere in the town the visitor is greeted by medieval houses and Baroque churches. In a corner of one of the squares is the postmaster's house of bygone days, from which the stagecoach left for Vienna, Pozsony and Pest. The town also harbours a castle, behind the walls of which Miklós Jurisich and his handful of brave men put up a heroic resistance against the Turkish army in 1532. The Strucc Hotel is also still standing, within whose thick walls Franz Liszt once lived.

We have now arrived in that part of the country where, regardless of the subject, the adjective "vasi" (say: woshy)

Two tasty dishes offered by the Windmill Tavern: Kuruc Pork Roast and Gourmet Chops (left). The Castle of Nagycenk (right). The Arany Strucc Hotel and the City Hall in Kőszeg (below).

is invariably used. The traditional local dress is "vasi", as are local humour and tastes. Above all, the word signifies a kind of spirit of tolerance that makes possible the perfectly harmonious blending of Hungarian, Austrian, and Slovene customs, traditions, dialects, and—it goes without saying—flavours.

The word "vasi" derives from the name of County Vas, to which the whole area belongs. The name, which, incidentally, denotes "iron", is in fact rather misleading. It comes from the name of a small town Vasvár, once the county seat. It served as the royal depot and distribution point for the crude iron produced in the region. However, this was all more than 600 years ago. Although the town itself still exists, the production of iron ceased long ago, and the county seat is no longer Vasvár but the much larger town of Szombathely. The term "vasi", however, has remained.

Making a small detour, I arrived at the little border village of Porlóapáti. It was there that I hoped to become acquainted with "vasi" cooking at its ancient original source. My first "encounter" took place at the home of Mrs. István Potzmann, the famous local cook. "Auntie" Potzmann cooks and bakes for the entire area—whenever special occasions arise. At weddings, Christenings, or other similar occasions at which people come together to celebrate with food and drink, Mrs. Potzmann is called upon to prepare the dishes and pastries.

My introduction to "vasi" cooking began with a delicately flavoured Chicken Soup. The chicken pieces had been cooked in soup stock, then skimmed and seasoned with salt and chopped parsley. The soup was thickened with sour cream, egg yolks and flour. The crowning touch was provided by the flavour of apples. Chopped and cooked separately and then gently blended into the soup, along with the liquid they had been simmered in.

The mildly seasoned chicken soup, which was most probably influenced by the cooking of neighbouring Austria, was a good prelude to the "Vasi" Pork Chops *(vasi pecsenye)*, this spicy dish being strictly in the tradition of Hungarian cuisine. The dish is a simple but tasty one. The pork chops are marinated overnight in milk seasoned with garlic. They are then dipped in a flour and paprika mixture and fried in hot lard to a golden brown. The tartness of the homemade dill pickles that Mrs. Potzmann served with the pork chops pleasantly complemented the hearty flavour of the meat.

Apples and sour cream give Aunt Potzmann's Chicken Soup its specially good and piquant taste (below).

The butchers of the Vas area have always been famous, not only throughout Hungary but in Austria and Bavaria as well. Vas cold-cuts on display (right).

Szombathely, a town with Vas atmosphere of nostalgia and charm. The ruins of the Temple of Isis built by the Romans in the 2nd century and a synagogue of the last century (above). Old houses in the main street of Szombathely (below). Ingredients for Tarragon Pork Roll (right).

The meat course was followed by two varieties of "vasi" strudel, reputedly of ancient origin. One of them was filled with highly seasoned mashed potatoes, while the other contained an egg filling enriched with sour cream. A double thickness of dough is used in making these strudels, which must be consumed while they are still fresh and quite warm.

After the village detour followed Szombathely, a town full of atmosphere and mellowed with age. Its precursor was a Roman town, and an "imperial" one at that time. During his travel to the region, Emperor Claudius recognized the importance of the location at the junction of the north-south and east-west roads, and it was he who ordered the establishment of the town in A.D. 43. Within half a century Claudia-Savaria became the capital of Upper Pannonia. Among the ancient relics that have been uncovered in the area are those associated with the Isis cult and also ones belonging to the early period of Christianity, including the remains of the 4th-century St. Quirinus Basilica. The side-chapel of the Dominican Church, legend has it, stands where Saint Martin's house of birth used to be, upholding Szombathely's right in the contest for the birthplace of the Gaul missionary bishop.

Despite the many beautiful old buildings, which line the streets and squares of the town's inner quarters, it would still not be appropriate to call Szombathely a town with an "historic" atmosphere. On the contrary, the capital of the "vasi" countryside is characterized by a contemporary spirit and an exuberant vitality. Take, for example, the main square in the center of town. For more than a decade now, city architects have been rebuilding it until finally it earned the approval of the local population. The residents of Szombathely envisioned the square not as an official place for holding public gatherings, but as a kind of lively "agora", where people could stroll, chat, shop, date, and—of course—eat and drink. In addition, they wanted the square to be pleasing to the eye, a kind of public park with flowers and shrubs. Obviously, it was no easy task to satisfy so many expectations.

Köztársaság tér (Republic Square), as the main square is officially called, has truly become a town center bubbling with life. It has also obviously become one of the focal points for the famous "vasi" gastronomy. Restaurants, cafés, and pastry shops abound, their terraces adorned with attractively covered tables in the shade of colourful parasols. A little further down the street is the Szombathely meat industry's superb delicatessen, with its superb selection of meats, cold cuts and various cold-buffet delicacies.

One of the sources of the delicious "vasi" flavours is obviously the area's outstanding animal husbandry. The fattened beef and pork, as well as the excellent poultry, provide the basis fort the "vasi" cooked dishes and cold cuts. A quick sampling of some of the items in the local meat shops confirmed that, apart from the basic ingredients used, some of the secrets of the local cooking are related to culinary know-how and the actual methods of preparation employed. One such example can be seen in the way in which *kolbász,* a sausage found all over Hungary, is prepared in "vasi" cooking. *Vasi szárazkolbász* is milder tasting than other Hungarian *kolbász,* because there is no paprika in it. In contrast to this, how-

ever, their *paprikás-kolbász* is even spicier than *gyulai kolbász*, the latter being noted for its spiciness elsewhere in Hungary.

While in Szombathely, I tasted the Pork "Cheese" *(mágnás sajt)*, a superb mixture of marinated ham and smoked pork leg, and the Pork Chop Roll *(karaj rolád)*, smoked pork loin stuffed with the earlier-mentioned *vasi szárazkolbász*. I also sampled Ham Mosaic *(sonka mozaik)*, a mixture of smoked Hungarian ham in aspic, and the Szombathely speciality as well as a host of cold-buffet masterpieces ranging from Pressed Poultry in Aspic *(szárnyasgalantin)* to Pork Loin with Breaded Stuffing. Centuries of tradition can be discerned behind the delicious flavours. In fact, "vasi" butchers have always been famous, not only throughout Hungary but in Austria and Bavaria as well.

After the appetizing preliminaries, a more thorough initiation into the world of "vasi" cooking ensued. The grand master of Szombathely chefs, Károly Varga, presented the *csiperkeleves*, a delicately spiced and mildly flavoured mushroom soup. For this dish, the mushrooms are sautéed in butter, rubbed through a sieve and added to meat stock. The soup is then thickened with a mixture of sour cream, egg yolk, and flour and seasoned with salt, pepper, and nutmeg. At the end of the cooking process, lemon juice and parsley are added and the soup is strewn with croutons before it is served, piping hot.

The subsequent course consisted of a dish called Tarragon Lubi Pork Roll *(tárkonyos lubi pecsenye)*. Credit for its

Pumpkin and Poppy Seed Strudel. The unusual combination of exciting flavours results in an excellent pastry (above and below).

popularity must go to a "vasi" chef of older times named István Gonda, who knew how to prepare the dish splendidly. Whether he was the originator of the dish or merely perfected it cannot be determined. Whichever the case may be, since that time it has spread throughout the Szombathely area and is the preferred dish for weddings, christenings and other festive occasions.

Tarragon Lubi Pork Roll is prepared in the following manner. Part of the pork leg is sliced into thin steaks, while the remainder is soaked in milk and then ground and made into a filling with breadcrumbs, liver, parsley, and, of course, tarragon. The filling is distributed evenly among the pork slices, which are then rolled up and browned a little in lard. The pork rolls are then cooked with onions and *lecsó* (a mixture of green peppers and tomatoes which is used in many Hungarian dishes). When well done, the meat is removed and the sauce thickened with sour cream. The meat is then returned to the mixture and heated to a boil. To make the tasty combination even more flavourful, pre-cooked smoked bacon slices are added to it, and the mixture is left to cook for a few minutes longer.

To make the "vasi" feast complete, Chef Varga prepared a special strudel for dessert: Pumpkin and Poppy-Seed Strudel *(tökös-mákos rétes)*. The name sounds as strange as the actual pairing of the ingredients used to make the excellent pastry. To prepare the dish, the pumpkin is grated, salted and then pressed or squeezed dry and sprinkled with sour cream. The poppy-seeds are minced and cooked, and sugar and raisins added to them. They are then cooled and added to the pumpkin. The resulting mixture is rolled up in the strudel dough, which is baked to a golden brown. The strudel is then dusted with powdered sugar and served warm.

HUNTERS' AND SHEPHERDS' FEASTS

László Hegyháti's main passion in life is hunting. Four days a week he goes to the Kemeneshát forest in pursuit of game. On the remaining three days, he runs the Pásztor Csárda. On those days when Hegyháti is out hunting, his wife Mária receives customers. It is not a bad division of labour, as Hegyháti's hunting expeditions provide the game for the following week's dishes. He brings back deer, wild boar and other such game as the hunting season permits.

The Hegyhátis are no ordinary married couple. The husband was famous as a champion equestrian. Mária, who studied economics, was a first-class basketball player.

Nor is the restaurant itself ordinary. Its walls are adorned with exotic hunting trophies from Hungary and elsewhere, all of which were shot by Hegyháti over the years. Among the trophies are deer and wild boar from the forests of western Hungary, as well as gnu and gazelle from Tanzania. The Pásztor Csárda derives its name from the fact that, in olden times, the shepherds from the surrounding area frequented the inn to drink wine and enjoy themselves in their free time. That was, of course, a very long time ago. Since that time, Szombathely expanded and thus the inn no longer stands alone in the middle of the forest, but is now situated on the outskirts of the town.

Harking back to the days of the past, lamb dishes are still served in the restaurant. Lamb in Paprika Sauce (*birkapaprikás*), cooked with white wine to make it even tastier, is offered with tiny Pinched Dumplings (*galuska*) and a side-dish of dill pickles. These days, however, gourmets frequent the inn for its game dishes, especially as it is rare to find a place that has its own huntsman. Unless otherwise stated the recipes in this book serve four people.

Choosing from among the many different game dishes offered by the Pásztor Csárda is no easy task. For a starter, I tried the Forester's Wife's Soup (*erdészné-leves*), which turned out to be a mushroom and sour-cream ragout prepared from venison. Mária then so graciously offered the Game Consommé (*erőleves vadhúsból*) that I sampled a few spoonsful from it as well. The soup also contains quail eggs which have been poached in it.

When it came to the wild boar, I was very lucky. Hegyháti had arrived home two days before with a young boar, which he prepared with sour cream. It was an exceptionally fine dish. The boar had been marinated in a little wine and hot butter to tenderize it. It was then baked and sprinkled with a little flour, after which it was basted with more wine and left to cook in its own juices. At the end of the cooking process, the sour cream was added and the dish delivered immediately to the table. It was a stroke of luck that I just happened to arrive there at the right moment to be able to savour some wild boar.

The roast young boar was a tremendous success. I didn't even mind having to turn down the roast boar made with red wine, which is similarly one of the choice dishes of the Pásztor Csárda. Moreover, one should not become

The Pásztorcsárda, with the trophies of its owner, László Hegyháti (above). Ingredients of the Braised Leg of Venison (below).

too attached to the wild boar while there are other wonderful dishes on the menu as well, such as Venison Liver, Hunter's Style *(őzmáj vadász módra)* and Braised Leg of Venison *(serpenyős szarvascomb)*. The leg of venison was braised with fried onions and seasoned with paprika and caraway seeds. Sliced tomatoes and green peppers were also added to the meat during the cooking process. It turned out to be one of the finest game dishes that I have ever eaten. It is true that this is also due to the exceptional quality of the game in that part of the country. Because of the superabundant vegetation which provides an excellent diet for the game, the meat tends to be richer in flavour than elsewhere.

A good local wine also added to the atmosphere. Among the abundance of wines available in the area, the Vaskereszti Burgundy, a beautiful garnet-coloured wine with a fiery quality, goes exceptionally well with game dishes.

STUFFED CAPON IN ŐRSÉG

"Őrség is the westernmost part of Hungary and juts into Austria and Yugoslavia in the shape of a peninsula. The mix of surrounding cultures has imparted a unique and interesting character to the area. Villages in the insulated valleys have preserved many of the folk traditions and customs—including local dress and architecture—that have already faded into oblivion elsewhere. Wooden belfries, hip-roofed peasant houses, and old press-houses yield picturesque scenes. Among the folk crafts of the area, pottery-making still flourishes in several places there.

The name of the area, which literally means "garrison", relates to its early role as a frontier. Following the Magyar conquest, the warlord Vér–Bulcsu stationed border guards there and the privileges bestowed on the population of the frontier zone survived for many centuries. This is the reason, apparently, why the villages developed in a unique fashion, forming clusters. In each small cluster of houses lived the members of one large extended family, the blood ties of which were closely intertwined.

This original mode of development has left its imprint on the area, even though the earlier isolation of the Őrség is now a thing of the past. Its beautiful scenery and multi-faceted folklore attract many tourists. And the cooking of the area is no less enticing.

In Magyarszombatfa, the so-called "potter's village", can be found beautifully designed jugs and plates, in addition to special cooking vessels. Food cooked in these earthenware pots retain all of their natural flavour and aroma. The cooking vessels appear to be directly descended from the clay cooking pots used by the Romans, although their shape differs and the Őrség pots have a glazed exterior. Such differences can, however, easily be explained by the fact that fifteen hundred years have elapsed since the Romans left Pannonia. In fact, it is remarkable that the Őrség potters still adhere to the old traditions, even if they are slightly modified or transformed.

Superb dishes are prepared in the Őrség earthenware pots. The delectable flavours and aromas of meat, vegetables, and smoked bacon all beautifully blend when baked together in the pot. One of the famous examples of such cooking is Clay-Baked Rabbit *(fazekas nyúl)*, which is prepared in the following manner. The rabbit is thoroughly rinsed, dried and cut up into serving pieces.

A farmstead in Őrség (preceding page). A typical Őrség peasant house in Pityerszer (below).

"Poor man's fare" but very tasty: Corn Pone, or Hoe Cake (right).

The bottom of the clay pot is covered with smoked bacon, on top of which is placed a layer of sliced potatoes, covered by a layer of meat, followed by a layer of sliced onions and sprinkled with salt and paprika. The entire process, with the exception of the bacon, is repeated until all of the meat has been used up, ending with a layer of onion, sprinkled with paprika. The pot is then covered and placed in the oven and left to bake for 3–3½ hrs, depending on the age of the rabbit. The real secret in preparing the dish, though, is that the pot must not be disturbed in any way after it is placed in the oven, and this includes not even adding a single drop of water to the meat.

It is well worth making an excursion from Magyarszombatfa to Velemér, and for several reasons. First of all, the setting is spectacular, as the village is located in the foothills of the Alps at the edge of an enormous forest which extends into Austria and Slovenia. Above the village, on the side of the mountain, stands one of the oldest churches in western Hungary. Its pointed arches are evocative of Gothic art, and in its interior is a 14th-century fresco depicting St. Ladislas, one of the canonized kings of the Árpád dynasty. The church was built in the second half of the 13th century.

Velemér, which harbours and preserves its ancient monuments, no longer, of course, lives in the past. The people of Őrség love to eat and drink, and in the kitchens of the peasant homes, housewives guard the secrets of wonderful dishes. Culinary activities are not limited, however, merely to the women of the household. There are some dishes that directly involve preparation on the part of the men, such as Mutton Cooked in a Cauldron (bográcsos ürühús), which is traditionally prepared in a large kettle over an open fire. The cauldron is lined with cabbage leaves, on which are placed sliced potatoes and the chunks of meat, generously seasoned. A little water is poured over the meat, and it is then left to stew until the entire contents of the pot are cooked. In all honesty, though, I should add that the more complicated dishes, which require more meticulous preparation work, are still, for the most part, made by the women. However, the women have also preserved a few frugal "poor man's dishes" among their collection of baking recipes, such as Hoe Cake, or Sweet Corn Pone and the renowned Őrség pretzels.

One of the Őrség specialties that I would particularly like to mention is Stuffed Capon (kappantekercs), as I had such a pleasant encounter with this dish and, moreover, had the good fortune to witness its preparation in the kitchen of one of the beautiful old Velemér peasant houses.

As soon as the capon was killed, the work began in earnest. A thin glass tube was inserted beneath its skin and air was forcefully blown into it in order to separate the skin from the flesh of the animal. The capon was then immediately plunged into scalding hot water and stripped of its feathers. A long incision was then made along its back, and the innards and meat carefully removed through the opening. Afterwards, the meat was minced and prepared into a filling mixed with diced bacon, chopped smoked tongue of pork, and mushrooms. The filling was then stuffed beneath the skin of the animal and the incision carefully sewn back together. The following step proved to be an unexpected and unusual one. The cook thoroughly buttered a clean linen

A young master of ancient pottery craftsmanship, Mrs. Erika Kovács Gács; stork nest carrying hay; In a farmxard Flowers im front of a peasant house; flowering chestnut trees in Cák; old draw-well; Imre Pető's famous basket weaving in Szalafő; wild mushrooms; Dániel Gömbös, a beekeeper from Őriszentpéter (left). Hay harvesting in Pankasz (below).

cloth and wrapped up the stuffed capon in it. The bundled bird was then lowered into a simmering stock, in which the smoked tongue had been boiled, and left to cook undisturbed. The capon was actually suspended in the pot by a wooden spoon, which had been inserted under the knot of the "bundle" and then laid across the rim of the pot. The bird was left to cook in the broth for about an hour, by which time it was judged to be "cooked to perfection". When the cook finally unwrapped the bundle, the most delectable aroma issued forth. It seems that the thick linen cloth is capable of preserving the flavour and aroma of the meat cooked in it. In fact, without the use of such a cloth, the Őrség stuffed capon would not be the "real thing".

Thus, thanks to the fine meat of the homebred capon and pork tongue used to make the dish, the delicate flavour of the wild mushrooms from the nearby forest, and the homespun cloth in which the bird was wrapped, but —above all—to the masterly skill of the cook, I was able to enjoy, in a little Őrség village, one of the finest dishes of my gourmet tour of western Hungary.

It was served with mashed potatoes, steamed cabbage, and an attractive-looking white wine, Italian Riesling *(Olaszrizling),* which went very well with the dish.

The delicious Stuffed Capon, accompanied by the refreshing tangy taste of the wine-and-soda drink, brought to a memorable and fitting end of my culinary adventures in the frontyard of the Alps, in Western Hungary.

Authentic Őrség Pretzels baked in an old-fashioned oven (above and below). Ingredients for Őrség Stuffed Capon (right). Farmyard (following page).

Butter an ovenproof dish and dust with breadcrumbs. Evenly distribute half of the bread and milk mixture in the bottom of the dish. Cover with the apples. Sprinkle the apples with ground walnuts and cinnamon. Top with the remaining bread and spread with half of the jam. Bake in a preheated moderate 180° C (350° F) oven for 25–30 minutes.

Beat the egg whites with the remaining powdered sugar, then gently fold in the remaining jam. Remove the pudding from the oven and pile the meringue mixture on top of it. Decorate with the grapes. Reduce oven temperature and return the pudding to the oven. Leave only long enough for the meringue to brown to a golden colour.

To serve, slice with a knife dipped in hot water.

CHESTNUT ROLL (GESZTENYÉS TEKERCS)

Cake:
300 g (10–11 oz) flour
150 g (5 oz) powdered sugar
6 eggs, separated
20 g (¾ oz) baking powder
20 g (¾ oz) vanilla sugar (or 1 tsp vanilla extract)
salt

Filling:
250 g (8–9 oz) chestnut purée
100 ml (4 fl. oz.) cream
2 tbsp rum
100 ml (4 fl. oz.) cherry brandy

Icing:
100 g (3½–4 oz) hazelnut or almond macaroons, ground
50 g (2 oz) butter
1 egg yolk
1 tbsp cocoa
100–200 ml (4–7 fl. oz.) whipped cream, for decoration
candied cherries or other candied fruit, for decoration

Beat the egg yolks and mix with the sugar and vanilla, then add the baking powder and flour. Beat the egg whites stiffly with a pinch of salt and gently fold into the mixture. Line an oblong, medium-sized baking tin with buttered waxed paper. Spread the mixture evenly on it and bake in a preheated moderate 180° C (350° F) oven for 15–20 minutes. While the cake is baking, prepare the filling by blending together the chestnut purée, rum and cream.

When the cake is done, turn it out onto a clean dish towel and splash immediately with the cherry brandy. Allow to cool 2–3 minutes, then spread the filling evenly over the cake. Roll up tightly and leave to cool completely. Beat the butter with the egg yolk and cocoa until frothy. Thinly coat the cooled chestnut roll with the frosting and sprinkle abundantly with the macaroons. Chill in the refrigerator.

To serve, decorate with whipped cream and candied fruit.

HOE CAKE OR SWEET CORN PONE (PRÓSZA OR TEJES MÁLÉ)

600 g (1¼ lb) fine-ground maize flour
1 l (1¾ pt) milk
3–4 tbsp sugar
100 g (3½–4 oz) butter or margarine
20 g (¾ oz) yeast
1 sugar cube
100 ml (4 fl. oz.) sour cream (½ cup)
1 egg
100 g (3½–4 oz) tart jam (cherry, plum etc.)
grated peel of one lemon

Pour 900 ml (1½ pt) of hot milk over the flour. Stir to blend and set aside to thicken for at least 1 hour. Culture the yeast in 50 ml (2 fl. oz.) of lukewarm milk in which the sugar cube has been dissolved. Combine with the thickened flour mixture. Add the sugar, sour cream, egg, grated lemon peel, and a pinch of salt.

Butter a deep baking dish or pan and spread the mixture evenly in it. Cover with a linen towel and set in a warm place to rise for one hour. At baking time, uniformly dot the surface with the jam and bake in a preheated hot 200° C (400° F) oven until browned. Cut the cake into squares, having a jam dot in the middle of each. Additional jam can be served with it in a separate dish.

ŐRSÉG PRETZELS (ŐRSÉGI PEREC)

1 kg (2–2¼ lb) flour
30 g (1 oz) yeast
1 tsp salt
400–500 ml (¾ pt) milk
2 sugar cubes

Dissolve the sugar in 100 ml (4 fl. oz.) of lukewarm milk. Add the yeast and blend. To prepare the leavening, beat in 3–4 tbsp of the flour, then leave to rise in a warm place. Add the mixture to the remaining flour. Add the salt and enough of the lukewarm milk to make a pliable dough. Knead the dough until smooth and bubbles form on the surface. Place in a deep bowl and dust the surface with flour. Cover with a clean tea towel and leave to rise until doubled in volume. On a floured pastry board, knead the dough gently and then divide into eight loaves. Roll out into long strips. Bringing the two ends together, shape each strip into a large pretzel. Cover with the tea towel and let rise once more. Bake the pretzels in a preheated 200° C (400° F) oven until brown. Do not open the oven door until the pretzels are ready or they will fall.

Notes: Upon removing the pretzels from the oven, baste with a damp pastry brush to produce a nice golden colour. The pretzels may be made with sour milk. Water must not be used!

Title of the original: Sopron környéki ízek
Corvina, Budapest, 1989

© Text: Zoltán Halász
© Photographs: Károly Hemző
The recipes were written by Mari Lajos
Design by Vera Köböl
Translated by Chris Tennant
Revised by Christina Rozsnyai

ISBN 963 13 2769 8
HU ISSN 0238-7166

Printed in Hungary, 1989
Kossuth Printing House,